Forgiveness

THE GREATEST HEALER OF ALL

GERALD G. JAMPOLSKY, M.D.

Forgiveness

THE GREATEST HEALER OF ALL

BEYOND
WORDS
Publishing
I N C

Beyond Words Publishing, Inc.
20827 N.W. Cornell Road, Suite 500
Hillsboro, Oregon 97124-9808
503-531-8700

Design: Principia Graphica
Composition: William H. Brunson Typography Services
Managing editor: Kathy Matthews
Editor: Hal Zina Bennett
Proofreader: Marvin Moore

Printed in the United States of America
Distributed to the book trade by Publishers Group West

Library of Congress Cataloging-in-Publication Data
Jampolsky, Gerald G., 1925–
    Forgiveness : the greatest healer of all / Gerald G. Jampolsky.
      p.   cm.
    ISBN 1-58270-020-6 (pbk.)
    1. Forgiveness.   2. Conduct of life.   I. Title.
  BJ1476.J35   1999
  179'.9—dc21   99-16386
                                                    CIP

The corporate mission of Beyond Words Publishing, Inc.:
Inspire to Integrity

This book is dedicated to my wife, soul mate, and life partner, Diane V. Cirincione, Ph.D., who has so strongly demonstrated and taught me what is beyond my imagination about the power of God's love and forgiveness in our life together.

CONTENTS

SIX
Miracles of Forgiveness

SEVEN
Stepping Stones to Forgiveness

Epilogue

FOREWORD

You are holding a book that will change your life. You've heard about such books, I'm sure. Perhaps you've even read one before. They're rare, it's true. In fact, given the number of books in print, they're very rare. But every so often one will present itself to you. I mean that literally. I mean, it will literally present itself to you.

Maybe it will be given to you as a gift. Or perhaps you'll hear about it from a friend. You might find it on someone's coffee table. Or it will be the only title that really catches your eye as you browse the bookstore.

Only you know how the book that's in your hands right now came to you, but I can tell you this: It did not come to you by accident. You are not reading it by chance. God brought this book to you. I am convinced of that. God does these things all the time. It's one of the ways God communicates with you when He's got something She wants you to hear or when you call out to the universe for an answer, for some insight, for some help with something that's troubling you.

I don't know if there's anything troubling you right now, or if you've been wishing for a little insight, or if it's just one of those times when God feels it would be good for you to hear something, but I do know that your having this book in your hands right now is perfect.

You'll see this, too, when you finish reading it. You'll know exactly why you picked it up.

Now let me tell you a little about the man who wrote this book. He's one of the most extraordinary men I have ever met. He's a man who carries peace and love and joy in his heart in such abundance that it spills over onto his face. You can see it in his eyes. You can feel it in his smile. And when he shakes your hand or gives you a big hug—he gives a lot of big hugs—you can feel that peace and joy and love going right through you.

That's the kind of man we're talking about. I know Jerry personally, and I've had those experiences. I'm telling you about him now because I think it's important for you to know something about the person who has placed this information before you. I want you to know that it comes from a highly credible source.

Not that Jerry Jampolsky needs an introduction or, certainly, any validation from me. His work over the years in creating the Center for Attitudinal Healing in the San Francisco Bay area and in fostering the establishment of over a hundred similar centers dotting the globe has won him the grateful admiration of people the world over. And his extraordinary book *Love Is Letting Go of Fear* stands today as one of the most significant texts on applied spirituality of the past half century. What I want you to know is not who Jerry *is* but rather that *he is who you would think he is* from reading his previous writings and observing his lifework—in other words, he is a man who walks his talk.

Why do I consider it important for you to know that? Not because I think Jerry needs or

wants the praise. Far from it. Rather, it's important for you to know what this man is like
because his life lived is evidence that *what he
teaches works*.

That's a tribute, because Jerry has had a lot of
stuff to overcome in his life. You don't have to be
told all about that here. It's enough to say that
his life has not been what you would call tidy. Yet
for over twenty years Jerry has been ministering
to the world and inspiring millions.

What caused this change in him? The same
thing that will cause a change in you—the subject
of this book: forgiveness.

Now let's get something clear about Jerry
Jampolsky. He's not perfect. No one who knows
him would tell you that. What they would tell you
is that he is perfectly clear that he's not perfect,
that no one is—and that this is his great healing
insight. He understands that we are all human,
that we all make mistakes, that we all can be hurtful or selfish, unkind or thoughtless. He knows
what it's like to wrestle with ego, to battle with fear,
and to struggle with love. He knows the deep inner
disappointment of wanting to be big, and still

acting small; of wanting to be gentle, and still acting harshly; of wanting to be wise, and still acting foolish.

He's had plenty of moments when he's been less than his grandest self. His special grace is that he would be the first person to tell you that. His special gift is that he'd be the first person to let you be less than perfect too—and get away with it.

You see, Jerry Jampolsky has come to understand some things about forgiveness. He's learned to forgive himself for all the times in his life when he's shown up as less than Who He Really Is, and he's learned to forgive others when they've done the same. Where this has brought Jerry is to a place of deep inner peace. It has given him a capacity to deal with those whom others would call "difficult people" with uncommon patience and unmatched equanimity. It has caused him to seek to practice unconditional love. It has allowed him to heal himself and others.

Now, you may not know, or be aware, that you have anything to heal. Or, in fact, you may have nothing to heal. (I would, frankly, be surprised if that were the case, because I have not met many people with no inner wounds to heal, but I will allow for the possibility.) Still, that will not stop you from healing others. And that is the real work you have been called to do here on this planet. We have all been brought here to heal each other—to heal each other of every false thought, of every small idea, of every limiting or fearful concept of ourselves that stops us from experiencing Who We Really Are. We've been given some marvelous tools with which to do that, and one of the most marvelous of all is forgiveness.

Forgiveness is capable of producing some of the most profound transformations you could ever hope for or imagine in your life and the lives of others.

Forgiveness can change everything—overnight. That's what's so exciting about it. It can change everything. It can bring joy where there is sorrow, peace where there is turmoil, gladness where there is anger. And it can give you back to yourself.

What I've noticed in my life is that it has been easier to talk about forgiveness than to practice it. That's why Jerry's book is so important to me. I am glad to learn more about this miracle tool and the miracles it can produce. I am so happy to learn how to use it and not just talk about it.

Let me end my commentary here by telling you one final thing about this book. This book is Jerry's truth, but it is God's message. God is just using Jerry as a communicator. So as you read this book, be very clear that you are having a conversation with God.

And be very sure that you are not having it by accident.

Neale Donald Walsch
Author of *Conversations with God*

ACKNOWLEDGMENTS

With my deepest appreciation, I wish to thank the many people who have come to the Center for Attitudinal Healing in Sausalito, California, as well as the many friends that my wife, Diane Cirincione, and I have met through the years who have taught us so much about forgiveness.

My warm and special thanks to my dear friend for many years, Hal Zina Bennett, Ph.D., who was so helpful in the final editing of this book.

I am especially grateful to Cynthia Black and Richard Cohn, as well as the rest of the Beyond Words staff, for their helpful comments, support, and encouragement in writing this book.

I wish also to acknowledge that some of the concepts in this book are my interpretations of the principles from *A Course in Miracles*. At times

I have paraphrased the *Course*, and once I have quoted from it directly. The paraphrases are noted with asterisks.

I am most grateful to Judith Skutch Whitson and Robert Skutch, of the Foundation for Inner Peace, for their permission to quote from the *Course*.

A Course in Miracles is published by the Foundation for Inner Peace, P.O. Box 598, Mill Valley, California 94942-0598.

INTRODUCTION

I wrote this book because I truly feel that we teach what we want to learn, and forgiveness is the most important lesson that I have to learn. So in a very real way, I wrote this book for myself as a reminder that I really do want to end the suffering I cause myself and others through my judgments and difficulties with forgiveness.

I know from the times that I have truly been able to grasp these lessons that forgiveness gives me a sense of personal freedom, hope, peace, and happiness which I get in no other way. But I also know that forgiveness is not one of those things which we ever complete in our lives. It is ongoing, always a *work in progress*. It is a never-ending process because as long as we are living in these bodies there is a part of us that is going to be tempted, again and again, to make judgments.

Not a day goes by, I must confess, that I don't stumble, that I don't catch myself being judgmental about others or myself. Sometimes it happens in seemingly mundane ways. One story which comes to mind is something that happened to me a while back when I was visiting the beautiful island of Molokai in Hawaii.

While taking my early-morning run along the edge of a golf course, I spied two beer cans that someone had tossed beside the path. As I saw them, I became really annoyed and judgmental. How could anyone be so thoughtless and insensitive as to trash this beautiful land in this way? I was incensed. How stupid and crass could a person be to toss their empty beer cans out the window and clutter up this paradise like this?

Running past the cans, I headed back toward the place where I was staying. I was really building up a whole scenario in my mind about the insensitive person who had done this. But then my inner voice stopped me: "Wait! Rather than making judgments like this, maybe you could go back and pick up those beer cans." No matter how they got there, wasn't it better to correct what had been done rather than holding these harsh, judgmental thoughts in my mind for the rest of the day?

Then I had a little argument with myself. If I went back to get the cans, I might be late for the appointment I had. Was it worth it to take the extra five minutes or so to pick up the cans and dispose of them properly?

At last, I turned back and picked up the cans. As I did so, the discomfort of those judgmental feelings I was having suddenly was replaced by a wonderful feeling of peace and joy.

As I continued my run back to my hotel, memories came flooding into my consciousness. I remembered the times in my youth when I had tossed trash out of the car window. I had done things just as crass and insensitive as this person who'd left his beer cans behind. In that instant, I could see that part of my judgments about this act was a projection of my own guilt and my own judgments of myself. Picking up the beer cans and depositing them in the garbage was more than doing something to honor the beauty of this island paradise; it was a lesson in releasing myself from the past and freeing myself from my own self-judgments.

The deeper lesson for me was that I did not have to leave the litter out on the land. Nor did I have to carry around the uncomfortable judgmental feelings I was having. Beyond that, I saw that my judgmental feelings were judgments about myself. The very process of forgiving the litterer freed me from feelings I carried around about my own past behavior.

That moment was a reminder to me of how healing forgiveness can be, of how it can release us from the past and deliver us to the joy of living fully in this moment. In everyday life, we tend to think of forgiveness as being little more than accepting a person's apology. Sometimes, just to be polite, we accept apologies when we really don't feel very forgiving. Or perhaps we cling to our grievances about the way a friend or loved one has let us down, believing that this is a way to protect ourselves. In our confusion about forgiveness, we not only hold on to what causes us pain, we also blind ourselves to what can heal us.

Perhaps one of the most difficult things for me has been that lack of forgiveness keeps me attached to incidents which happened in the past. Whenever I cling to past grievances, I condemn myself to the darkness. Had I clung to the past and held on to my judgmental thoughts about those beer cans, the chances are pretty good that they'd still be lying beside the path back in Molokai—and I would still be feeling uncomfortable about my own judgments of myself.

Forgiveness releases us from so much. It stops our inner battles with ourselves. It allows us to stop recycling anger and blame.

Forgiveness allows us to know who we truly are. With forgiveness in our hearts, we can at last experience our true essence as love.

Forgiveness is the great healer that allows us to feel joined and at one with each other and all that is life.

Forgiveness has the power to heal both our inner and outer lives. It can change how we see ourselves and others. It can change how we experience the world. It can bring an end, once and for all, to the inner conflicts that so many of us carry around with us every moment of every day.

Imagine the peace that could come to our planet if all the people of the world would let go of old grievances with their neighbors. Imagine what could happen if we would all let go of centuries-old battles over racial differences, religious differences, and past injuries to one another!

As a physician for more than forty years, I can recall people with a variety of illnesses—from back problems, to ulcers, to high blood pressure, and even to cancer—who have had many of their symptoms abate as they learned to forgive. I have been heartened in recent years to see research emerging that shows a relationship between forgiveness and health. We now know that lack of forgiveness—that is, clinging to anger, fear, and pain—does have a measurable impact on our bodies. These create tensions which affect the physiological systems that we are dependent on for health. They affect the circulation of blood in our bodies. They affect the efficiency of our immune systems. They put stress on our hearts, on our brains, and on virtually every organ in our bodies. Lack of forgiveness is indeed a health factor.

I think about my own alcoholic years. Drinking was my way of deadening myself to the pain of my own self-judgments and judgments of others. That way of dealing with these feelings became a source of stress for me and everyone around me. Had I continued this pattern, I would have surely increased the conflicts with both my inner and outer lives. In time, I might have developed a serious physical disorder such as liver disease, cancer, digestive problems, or heart disease.

Twenty-five years ago, the first Center for Attitudinal Healing came into being. It started out as a safe place to support children facing catastrophic illnesses and soon expanded to include adolescents and adults. Based on some of the principles of *A Course in Miracles*, the primary goal of the group members, as well as the staff, board, facilitators, and volunteers, is to find inner peace as a way to create true health and to heal by letting go of fear. Even at those times when they could do nothing to change the conditions of their bodies, they were able to heal the feelings of anger, betrayal, unfairness, and fear of having a serious health condition. And it is often through forgiveness that they find themselves released from their fears and discomforts so that they can go on to live creative, productive, and happy lives. Today, the Center has 120 sister centers around the world, using the principles of Attitudinal Healing for a variety of human challenges, from relationship problems, to living with serious illness, to healing conflicts within families and organizations.

Forgiveness continues to be a core teaching at these free centers. And it continues to bring comfort and freedom to people's lives even when they are faced with the most grievous of circumstances. It is out of the years of hearing thousands of healing stories that this little book you now hold in your hands was inspired. Having witnessed so much healing that has come by the practice of Attitudinal Healing, I am convinced of the unequalled power of forgiveness. As we change our minds, we are led to a place of peace regardless of the challenges life has given us.

The Forgiveness Reminders at the end of each chapter can be used as daily meditations. You might find it helpful to write a Forgiveness Reminder on a piece of paper or card and carry it with you, referring to it several times throughout the day.

It is my hope that you, the reader, will find in these pages a way to experience more happiness, peace, and freedom in your life. We are on this journey together. It is my belief and conviction that through practicing the ongoing process of forgiveness we all might take part in bringing greater joy and peace not only into our own lives but into the lives of everyone around us.

What we need to forgive in others

may be something in ourselves

that we have hidden from

our awareness.*

We can choose to have peace

of mind as our only goal.*

We are responsible for

our own happiness.*

TO THE READER

As you read this book, consider keeping a small notebook or journal close at hand. You'll find it useful for making a record of any notes or insights that come to mind.

I'd like to suggest that a good place to start your journal entries is with a list of people who might be forgiven. Include on this list people who you presently feel should never be forgiven. To save some time in this process, I've tried to think of some of the different possibilities that might come up. The following should make it a little easier to choose who you might include on your list.

Parents, stepparents, family members, and relatives. Many of us grew up feeling that our parents did not give us exactly what we wanted or needed when we were children. At our lectures and workshops, Diane and I often ask for a raise of hands to show how many people have totally forgiven their parents. It is rare that more than 50 percent have done so.

In some cases, there was emotional, spiritual, physical, or sexual abuse which left scars that seem like they may never heal. In other cases, it might seem that you had a rather gentle, protective home environment when you were growing up, but you still feel hurt by things that happened. Even if you presently feel that what happened in your childhood is unforgivable—or maybe just bewildering—jot down any names that might come under this heading.

Spouses, ex-spouses, and past love relationships. In our workshops throughout the world, we often ask people to raise their hands if they have been divorced. Then we ask those people to raise their hands if they have *totally* forgiven their ex-spouses. Less than 25 percent of them raise their hands—which leaves 75 percent who have not forgiven an ex-spouse.

There is no doubt that forgiving an ex-spouse can be difficult. Presumably, these are people who we have once taken into our hearts and trusted. The pain, disappointment, or sense of betrayal and hurt that we feel can be quite deep. Even if you presently feel that they should never be forgiven or that you don't feel it is possible to do so, at least put their names on your list.

Authority figures. Many of us have had the experience of being let down, injured, deceived, disappointed, lied to, or even abused by people we feel we should have been able to trust in some aspect of our lives, such as teachers, religious leaders, foster parents, helping professionals, public officials, politicians, government leaders, manufacturers, retailers, and service providers. Government leaders, for instance, are sometimes responsible for horrible outrages against humanity—we have only to remember World War II and the Holocaust for proof of this. Similarly, there are times when professionals we pay to help us sometimes cause embarrassment or even serious injury. It may certainly seem that these people are the most unforgivable of all since we have entrusted them to serve the public. Once again, put their names on your list even if you are absolutely convinced that they should never be forgiven.

Your physical body. Are you totally at peace with your body? Or are you unhappy about the way it looks or feels? Do you have a physical challenge that is genetic or perhaps is caused by an illness or injury? Are you suffering from a serious illness? Are you unhappy about something that limits you from doing things which you would like to be able to do? Or are you angry that your body is aging and there is nothing you can do to stop the process? If any of these things are true for you, briefly describe them and put them on your list.

Your own past or present thoughts, feelings, and behaviors. Many of us have judgments about ourselves. We may find it difficult to accept a certain behavior that we seem to repeat again and again, no matter how much we try to change. We may have done things in the past that caused others injury or pain. We may feel that no matter how much time and energy we put into having a better relationship with a friend or family member, we cannot make things better. We may feel that we keep falling short of doing better at our job or moving toward a special goal. Or we may feel that we should be more generous toward other people—or less judgmental and more forgiving! No matter what it is, describe it briefly and put it on your list.

Acts of God, fate, luck, a higher power, the stars, or life itself. At times it can seem that life itself is against us. We often hear phrases like "I never have any luck!" or "It's just my fate!" or "If there is a God, how could God allow this to happen?" or "It's all in my stars!" Certainly there are times when we are angry with forces that seem bigger than ourselves or that appear to be beyond our control. Jot down any of these that might apply to you.

Accidents, offenses, and misdeeds of strangers. Life can at times seem to be filled with problems or even dangers that come about through nothing we have done. Whether it happens to be a traffic accident, a stranger's insult, or a burglar entering our house and making off with a valuable possession or an object with sentimental value for us, such grievances can also seem unforgivable. Add them to your list.

Reflections about Completing Your List

As you are completing your list, it is likely that a number of thoughts and questions will enter your mind. Here are just a few things that may come up:

- I feel afraid to forgive this person. If I do, aren't I condoning what they have done? Isn't forgiving going to send them the message that I am agreeing with them?

- I feel that because of the injury I have suffered, there is a barbed-wire fence around my heart—or my heart is like stone, and I can never change the hardness I experience when I think about this person.

- I vacillate between wanting to get even with this person for injuring me and wanting to erase the whole thing from my memory.

- I can never forgive myself for what I did, and I deserve to never be happy again.

- I would love to be able to let go of these hateful feelings I carry around for this other person, but I am afraid that if I let them go I can be hurt again.

- I am quite certain that I would feel much happier after letting go of this grievance, but I can't even imagine how to do that.

Questions and reflections such as these naturally come up for many of us as we sit down to list people and situations that we might forgive. There are no quick and easy answers to these questions. But this book was written with the hope and conviction that it might help readers take a closer look at the nature of forgiveness. It is about looking at the advantages and disadvantages of letting go of the grievances that we have encountered in our lives. As you will soon discover, the list you have just completed will help you focus on the realities of how forgiveness might work in your life.

Forgiveness means seeing the light

of God in everyone—regardless

of their behavior.*

The happiest marriages are built on a foundation of forgiveness.

One

The Roots of Unhappiness

Why is it so difficult for us to see that our search for the pot of gold at the end of the rainbow is only hiding the fact that we are both the rainbow and the gold?

Consider for a moment that happiness is our natural state of being. At the Center for Attitudinal Healing, where forgiveness is so much a part of everything that we do, we say that the essence of our being is love.* We learn to look at life from the perspective that we are spiritual beings who are just temporarily in these bodies of ours. When we look upon our lives that way, we also begin to see that love and happiness are inseparable. And what forgiveness teaches us is that it is possible to choose love over fear and peace over conflict regardless of the circumstances affecting our lives.

Before we talk about forgiveness, let's briefly explore the roots of unhappiness. By looking at where unhappiness starts, we can move toward a very different way of looking at the world. A good place to begin this exploration is with that part of us which believes that our happiness lies in external things.

Living in this modern society, as we do, it becomes all too easy to believe that money and the accumulation of material things will make us happy. The trouble is that the more we accumulate, the more we want. No matter how much we get, it almost never seems like enough. Once we begin making choices from this perspective, we fall into the habit of believing that we will eventually find something outside ourselves that will bring us lasting happiness. The fact that this search frequently ends up with our feeling frustrated, angry, unhappy, and even hopeless is our clue that this belief isn't working.

Why is it so difficult for us to see that our search for the pot of gold at the end of the rainbow is only hiding the fact that we are both the rainbow and the gold?

There are so many temptations in the world on which to blame our unhappiness or our lack of money and material things. We look around us and see people with more than we have who seem to be happier than we are. We turn to other people and seek to fill the hole in our souls with our relationships. It may seem like a big jump we are making from seeing more material things as the answer to seeing other people as the answer. But the same part of us which tells us that the answers are to be found in externals also tells us that we should be able to make other people responsible for our happiness. Surely, if we could only find the right person, our lives would be fulfilled!

Pretty soon we are on a psychological treadmill, going round and round in an endless circle, disappointed and unhappy because neither money and material things nor our relationships are making us happy. We have moments, but they seem too fleeting. We may begin to feel trapped by life. But what, we may ask, is the alternative?

What is this part of ourselves that keeps us seeking outside ourselves? Can we even name it? It is the part of us which believes that our true identity is limited to our bodies and personality self. It is the part of us which sneers at any suggestion that our true essence is that we are spiritual beings living for a time in these bodies.

I like to use the term *ego* to describe the part of us that is so concerned with externals. The ego tries to justify its presence in our lives by saying that it is only looking after our better interests, that our bodies need it to stick around or we are going to accidentally step out in front of a speeding truck or forget to feed ourselves or protect ourselves from all the dangers that are in the world. Our egos would have us believe that anyone who doesn't think that money can buy happiness doesn't know where to shop.

Again and again, our egos send us the message that we live in an unfair world where we will be victims if we aren't constantly on the alert. Our egos are quite happy when we become convinced of our victimhood, because then we hand our power over to them. The last thing our egos would want us to believe is that we have a choice—that we can choose not to be victims, that we can, in fact, choose love rather than fear, that we can choose to forgive rather than hold on to our embitterments, grudges, and judgments.

It is easy to see how the ego interprets happiness, love, and peace of mind as its enemies, for when we are enjoying these states of being, we are experiencing our spiritual essence. We are seeing a world that is very different from the one our egos furnish us. Forgiveness is easy when we look at the world through the eyes of love, since it is then clear that the answers we have been seeking all of our lives can be found here and not in the ego's beliefs in the externals of life.

At its worst, we hear the ego in our minds saying that it is impossible to experience happiness for long, so we had better be able to turn to the physical reality for our true and lasting happiness. Eventually, things will fall apart. Something is sure to go wrong. Someone or something will intrude on our happiness. So we'd better be on the lookout for the person who is to blame. The ego's advice is to become a faultfinder, to make certain we are always right and the other person is always wrong.

Ultimately, our happiness or unhappiness actually *is* measured by the degree to which we accept the advice of our egos. Think about what happens whenever we judge other people, hold grievances in our mind, or cling to blame and guilt. What we feel at such times blocks us from experiencing love, peace, and happiness. Our feelings of unhappiness are magnified and we become faultfinders, probing our world for circumstances or people who might be to blame for our unhappiness.

Forgiveness is a transformational process. In a heartbeat, we can let go of the externally based paradigm that says we must look outside ourselves for true happiness. With a simple change of mind, we can release ourselves from the ego's conviction that to be safe we must believe in our victimhood and act defensively. With a shift of perspective, we can stop seeking other people or things outside ourselves to blame for our unhappiness. We can embrace our true spiritual essence and instantly find that this has always been our source of love and peace and happiness. It is never more than a heartbeat away, and it is free for the asking.

Forgiveness can be learned at any age and by anyone, regardless of their present belief system, the past they have experienced, or the way they have treated others around them.

A Model for Forgiveness

Several years ago, my wife, Diane, and I met a remarkable woman by the name of Andrea de Nottbeck. We became acquainted with her through a most unusual phone call from a person in Switzerland, who told us that a woman who lived there had a painting she wanted to give us. The woman was ninety-three years old at the time and was very healthy. While she had given most of her wealth to philanthropic organizations, she still had one material possession to give away before she died. It was a thirteenth-century painting of Jesus Christ.

Feeling perplexed about who should get the painting when she died, Andrea had gone out to the mountains to meditate on it. After a few moments, she had gotten the message "*Love Is Letting Go of Fear.*" The painting, she decided, should go to Jerry Jampolsky, the author of the book by this title, which is about the ways that we prevent ourselves from loving. And so she had her friend call me in the States.

We learned that following her husband's death, several years before, Andrea had become a bitter, crotchety old woman. She was difficult to get along with, frequently provocative, and extremely argumentative. At the age of eighty-five, a friend gave her a copy of *Love Is Letting Go of Fear.*

This book became Andrea's daily reading. Soon she began forgiving all the people in her life who she felt had hurt her. She forgave herself for behavior she knew had caused pain or had been unloving. Miraculously, her life changed. No longer crotchety and angry at the world, she became more carefree and joyful than she'd ever been in her life. To celebrate her transformation, she changed her name to Happy.

Without my ever knowing it until I met Happy, she had been responsible for getting *Love Is Letting Go of Fear* translated and published in French many years before.

When I heard the story of Happy's transformation, Diane and I decided to visit her, combining our trip with one I already had scheduled for the Middle East. Upon our arrival, we met this most extraordinary woman. She showed us a French magazine with her picture on the cover—of her flying in a hang glider high over the French countryside! She was eighty-eight at the time. And as if that weren't enough, she had gone stunt flying in a biplane at the age of ninety-one.

We spent three wonderful days with Happy at her home in Geneva, Switzerland. I have to say that she lived up to her new name in every way imaginable. She was one of the happiest, most peaceful, and most loving people I have ever met.

When we asked Happy what she had done to bring about all these positive changes in her life, she replied, "Oh, I just gave up all my judgments."

We left Happy's home just after the first of the year, having celebrated the New Year with her. Diane took the painting she had given us back to California while I went on to my meeting with some friends in the Middle East. Three weeks later, we received a phone call that Happy had died peacefully in her sleep as she had predicted.

To this day I think about Happy's story of how her life was transformed through forgiveness. I am so grateful that I had the opportunity to meet this delightful woman. She will forever remain a most powerful model of forgiveness for both Diane and me, and a reminder to us all that we are never too old to change.

Miracles Inspired by Forgiveness

Finally, there is a story in Yitta Halbertstam and Judith Leventhal's book, *Small Miracles: Extraordinary Coincidences from Everyday Life*, which clearly illustrates the process of forgiveness. I paraphrase it here:

There was a young man named Joey, who at the age of nineteen left home and turned his back on his Jewish religion. His father was extremely upset with his son and threatened him with total rejection if he did not change his mind.

Joey did not change his mind, however, and all communication between father and son ceased. The son wandered throughout the world to find himself. He fell in love with a wonderful woman, and for a while he felt that his life had meaning and purpose.

A few years went by, and one day in a coffeehouse in India, Joey ran into an old friend from his hometown. His friend and he passed the time of day, and then the friend said, "I was so sorry to learn about your father's death last month."

Joey was stunned. It was the first he'd heard about his father's passing. He returned home and began to reexamine his Jewish roots. His girlfriend and he split up because she was Jewish, too, but did not want anything to do with her Jewish tradition.

After a short stay at home, Joey traveled to Jerusalem and found himself at the Wailing Wall. He decided to write a note to his deceased father, expressing his love and asking for his forgiveness.

After Joey wrote the note, he rolled it up and tried to fit it into one of the holes in the wall. In the process, another note fell out of the same hole and landed at his feet. Joey reached down and picked it up. Curious, he unrolled the note. The handwriting looked familiar. He read on. Amazingly, the note was from his father, asking God to forgive him for rejecting his son and expressing deep, unconditional love for Joey.

Joey was thunderstruck. How could this possibly happen? It was more than a coincidence—it was a miracle. As difficult as it was for him to believe what had occurred, there was the note, written in his father's own hand, irrefutable proof that this was not just a dream.

Joey began studying the Jewish faith in earnest. A couple years later, back in the States, a rabbi who was a friend of his invited him to dinner. That night at the rabbi's house, Joey came face-to-face with his old girlfriend who had left him years before. She, too, had returned to her Jewish roots.

And, yes, Joey and his girlfriend were married soon afterward.

Time and again we hear stories in which the process of forgiveness wipes clean the slate of a painful past. It is not always easy to accept the fact that a shift in perception can apparently produce such miracles, removing the blocks to our awareness of love. But Joey's story indicates that not even death can stand in the way of this process. It is as if the reality of the incident that once caused us such grief vanishes and is replaced by the love that was always there—and will always continue to be there forever and ever.

To not forgive is a

decision to suffer.*

*To be happy, all I have to do
is give up my judgments.**

Forgiveness is the most

powerful healer of all.*

$\mathcal{T}_{wo}$

What Is Forgiveness?

---

*We will truly have more peaceful
relationships when we stop telling
others how to live and start
practicing love and forgiveness.*

From the perspective of Love and Spirit, forgiveness is the willingness to let go of the hurtful past. It is the decision to no longer suffer, to
heal your heart and soul. It is the choice to no
longer find value in hatred or anger. And it is
letting go of the desire to hurt others or ourselves because of something that is already in
the past. It is the willingness to open our eyes to

the light in other people rather than to judge or condemn them.

To forgive is to feel the compassion, gentleness, tenderness, and caring that is always within our hearts, no matter how the world may seem at the moment. Forgiveness is the way to a place of inner peace and happiness, the way to our soul. That place of peace is always available to us, always ready to welcome us in. If, for the moment, we don't see the welcome sign, it is because it is hidden by our own attachment to anger.

Somehow, there is a part of us that believes we can get the peace of mind we seek by holding on to hatred, or anger, or pain. There's a part which says that we must protect ourselves and that we can achieve happiness and peace of mind by being attached to hatred and seeking revenge. There's a part of us that says we must withdraw and withhold our love and our joy because we have been hurt in the past.

We can look upon forgiveness as a journey across an imaginary bridge from a world where we are always recycling our anger to a place of peace. That journey takes us into our own spiritual essence and the heart of God. It takes us into a new world of expanding, unconditional love.

Through forgiveness, we receive all that our hearts could ever want. We are released from our fear, anger, and pain to experience oneness with each other and our spiritual Source.

Forgiveness is the way out of darkness and into the light. It is our function here on earth, allowing us to recognize ourselves as the light of the world. It allows us to escape the shadow of the past, whether that shadow is our own or another person's.

Forgiveness can free us from the imprisonment of fear and anger that we have imposed on our minds. It releases us from our need and hope to change the past. When we forgive, our wounds of past grievances are cleansed and healed. Suddenly we experience the reality of God's love. In that reality, there is only love, nothing else. In that reality, there is never anything to forgive.

In *A Course in Miracles*, there is a beautiful passage about forgiveness. I quote it here because it describes the benefits that can be ours through forgiveness:

"FORGIVENESS OFFERS
EVERYTHING THAT I WANT"

What could you want that forgiveness cannot give? Do you want peace? Forgiveness offers it. Do you want happiness, a quiet mind, a certainty of purpose, and a sense of worth and beauty that transcends the world? Do you want care and safety, and the warmth of pure protection always? Do you want a quietness that cannot be disturbed, a gentleness that never can be hurt, a deep abiding comfort, and a rest so perfect it can never be upset?

All this forgiveness offers you, and more. It sparkles on your eyes as you awake, and gives you joy with which to meet the day. It soothes your forehead while you sleep, and rests upon your eyelids so you see no dreams of fear and evil, malice and attack. And when you wake again, it offers you another day of happiness and peace. All this forgiveness offers you, and more.*

(FROM LESSON 122)

_____

Forgiveness is letting go of all

hopes for a better past.

_____

*The power of love and forgiveness in our lives can produce miracles.**

The key word in learning to forgive

is the willingness _to forgive._*

Three
The Unforgiving Mind

*Most of us would avoid taking drugs
that we know have detrimental side
effects. Yet much of the time we are not
very selective about the thoughts that we
put in our minds—nor are we aware
of the toxic effects these thoughts
can have on our bodies.*

Back in chapter one, I spoke of that part of ourselves which sees us as only a body and a personality. It is the part which tells us that our happiness is found in the external world through the accumulation of *things*. It is the part which tells us that if we could only find the right relationship to be in, everything in our lives would be perfect. And it is the part which believes that when things go wrong, the only reasonable thing to do is to find someone or some situation to blame. We called this part of us *ego*.

It can be helpful to think of the ego as having a belief system of its own. If we want, we can accept its beliefs or seek other ways of looking at the world. Of course, we have to remember that our egos are part of who we are. The greater our ability to recognize our fearful ego, the freer we are to choose a more loving and peaceful life.

Think of the ego's thought system as being based on fear, guilt, and blame. If we were to choose only to follow its guiding principles, we would always be in a state of conflict, and any peace or happiness that we might have will completely elude us.

Given that this is the way the ego works, it should come as no surprise that it does not believe in forgiveness. In fact, it will do everything it can to convince us that nobody in the world deserves our forgiveness. It even goes a step further than this and says that we do not deserve forgiveness ourselves! It clings fiercely to the belief that people do things for which they must never be forgiven.

The ego does, however, believe that we must constantly defend ourselves. It communicates this to us in feelings that we can easily recognize. For example, the unforgiving mind of the ego would try to convince us that the only way to protect ourselves from further harm is to punish the other person with our anger and our hatred, withdrawing from them so that they will feel bad for what they have done.

Our egos show up for us in the feeling that we would be foolish, stupid, or just plain insane to forgive this person whose actions have in some way hurt or threatened us. And if that were not enough, our egos remind us that there are people in our lives who are quite willing to nudge us and say that such-and-such a person hurt us and deserves our anger, not our forgiveness.

Of course, our egos are very clever. They know how to pick and choose their witnesses. And you can be sure that they have a good eye for selecting only those who totally agree with them. The friends I pick today, now that I am on a spiritual path, are quite different from the ones I had around me during those days when I was addicted to alcohol.

The ego is filled with contradictions. It has to hide from us, for example, the fact that when we hold on to our anger to punish others, we imprison ourselves. Another secret it has to keep is that our unforgiving thoughts create a hole in our hearts, not only causing a sense of loss and sadness but keeping us from experiencing inner peace and love. That hole separates us from each other and from our spiritual connection with each other.

If you believe in God, the ego may be busy telling you that your God is judgmental and angry. The ego may be busy telling you that God is ready to drop a brick on you to punish you for your misdeeds and "wrong" thoughts. The ego may be busy telling you that you cannot trust or feel safe with God.

The ego frequently tries to tell you that unconditional love from God is nothing but an illusion which you create and that as long as you hold on to this silly notion, you are deceiving yourself.

Our egos would have us believe that God is truly wrathful and ready at a moment's notice to cause people to die, to create natural disasters such as earthquakes and tornadoes that kill many people and leave them homeless. The ego would even have us believe that these are ways to punish people for misdeeds and wrong thoughts.

The unforgiving mind of the ego always has a good stock of fear, misery, pain, suffering, despair, weariness, and doubt. It is a mind that views mistakes as sins that should never be forgotten.

Possible Toxic Side Effects of Our Thoughts

Physicians try to be aware of the possible side effects of the medications they prescribe to their patients. And in this day as patients take greater responsibility for their own health, most of us also educate ourselves with that kind of information. If we are to free ourselves of the burden and discomfort of our grievances, we need to look just as carefully at the thoughts we put in our minds as we do at the drugs we put in our bodies. The side effects of holding unforgiving thoughts in our minds can have a very negative impact on our well-being. Take a look at the following list. Here are just a few of the physical problems that may be associated with an unforgiving mind:

- Headaches

- Backaches

- Pains in the neck

- Stomachaches and ulcer-like symptoms

- Depression

- Lack of energy

- Anxiety

- Irritability

- Tenseness and being "on edge"

- Insomnia and restlessness

- Free-floating fear (fear not attached to any particular event)

- Unhappiness

Few of us would ever take drugs that we know can hurt us. Yet we are not nearly as selective about the thoughts that we put in our minds. What is the antidote? What is the most powerful medicine we have for healing the thoughts that cause this long list of symptoms? Forgiveness. It is a powerful, amazing, and miraculous healer, with the capacity for making all these symptoms disappear.

The unforgiving mind hides from

our awareness the fact that we

imprison ourselves by holding

on to anger and hate.*

––––––––––––––––––

Forgiving others is the first step

to forgiving ourselves.*

––––––––––––––––––

Our immune systems can become

stronger when we forgive.

Four

The Top Twenty Reasons Why We Don't Forgive

There is always a choice to be made:
We can listen to the voice of love
*or to the voice of the ego.**

It is difficult to forgive when we listen to the advice of the ego, which tells us that we are doing the healthy thing by punishing the person who has hurt us and withholding our love from them. It is difficult to forgive because we have stubborn egos which attempt to convince us that it is better and safer for us to hate than to love.

It is important that we do not make our egos the enemy or be attached to their advice. But it is equally important to recognize that our egos lead us astray. Our egos preach to us constantly. They cling to a belief system that makes fear, conflict, indifference, and unhappiness top priorities, and they insist that expressing love is just insane.

I like to think differently—that perhaps we are really insane only when we are *not* allowing ourselves to experience and express our love.

When we become attached to listening to the voice of the ego, which we are especially prone to do during times of stress or when things are not going as we'd like, we will hear or feel in our minds the silent messages that tell us not to forgive.

There is always a choice to be made: *We can listen to the voice of love or to the voice of the ego.** How can we tell when it is the ego talking? The voice of the ego always comes from fear. It leaves us in a state of conflict, not peace. When we listen to the unforgiving mind of the ego, it will give us countless reasons why we should not forgive, always hiding the fact that when we don't forgive we are the ones who suffer and lose our sense of peace.* Here are twenty examples of the ego's reasoning:

1. That person really hurt you. They deserve your anger, your withdrawal of love, and any other punishment they get.

2. Don't be a fool! If you forgive, that person is just going to do the same damn thing all over again.

3. You are weak if you forgive.

4. If you forgive that person, it is the same as making them right and you wrong!

5. Only a person with really low self-esteem would ever consider forgiving that person.

6. When you don't forgive, it is like controlling the other person. Control is the ego's best way to keep safe.

7. The best way to keep a distance between yourself and the person who hurt you is to never forgive them.

8. Hold back your forgiveness since it is a way to feel good, knowing it is a good way to get your revenge.

9. Withholding forgiveness gives you power over the person who has hurt you.

10. Forgiving people who hurt you is just plain stupid.

11. If you forgive, you abandon all sense of security.

12. If you forgive someone, they might think you agree with what they did or didn't do.

13. Forgiving is nothing more than condoning bad behavior.

14. If push comes to shove, you should forgive the person only if they offer you a sincere apology—and then, only *sort of forgive*.

15. If you forgive, God will strike you down.

16. Let's face it—it's always the other person's fault, so why forgive?

17. Don't ever believe anyone who tries to tell you that you abhor things in other people which you can't stand to look at in yourself.

18. Don't fall for the idea that if you can't forgive something which another person has done, it's because you can't accept the fact that you have done something you consider unforgivable.

19. If you forgive that horrible act, you are no better than the person who is to blame!

20. You'll know you've really lost it with this forgiveness thing when you start believing that there is a God or Higher Power which protects you from being an innocent victim and getting yourself hurt.

What to Do with Ego Messages

Take some time to get acquainted with this list of ego statements. Soon you will recognize them when they come up in your own thoughts. At that point, you will recognize that you have a choice between the voice of the ego and the voice of love, the voice of forgiveness. In the coming chapters, we will explore ways to better hear this voice.

Forgiveness releases us

from the painful past.*

You either totally forgive or

you do not forgive at all.*

To forgive,

have a willingness to give

_all your anger and anguish to God._*

Five

Removing the
Obstacles to Forgiveness

---

*We can choose the thoughts
we put in our minds.**

Any time we pick up the newspaper or turn on
the evening news, we learn about all the shock-
ing situations that are happening in the world—
and even in our own backyards. It is easy to feel
quite convinced that some things which occur
are simply unforgivable. We might even feel
that we ourselves have done or said things in
our own lives that are unforgivable. But there is
a powerful message here—and it is that only

through forgiveness can we stop the cycles of destruction and pain on our planet.

Changing Our Belief Systems

If we are to learn the value of forgiving—of forgiving everyone, including ourselves—we need to change these belief systems. We can begin by letting go of the ego's belief that we must find someone to blame whenever something goes wrong. We can take new beliefs into our hearts, ones that allow us to see the value of letting go of self-condemnation and condemnation of others and surrendering to love.*

One of the ways we can do this is by changing how we think about who and what we are. The ego identifies us totally with the physical body instead of seeing us as spiritual beings who have come to live for a time in physical bodies. If we can adopt a willingness to look upon ourselves and each other as eternal spiritual beings and not just as bodies, it becomes much easier to see the value of forgiveness.

As I look back on my own life, I find that what kept me from experiencing peace of mind was my unwillingness to see the value of forgiving myself and others. I was caught in a whirlpool of shame and guilt and denial and anger about things that had happened in the past. For many years I saw myself as a victim. I blamed the world and everyone in it for my own unhappiness.

My own spiritual journey began in 1975 when I was introduced to *A Course in Miracles*. Those writings have made a remarkable difference in the way I view myself and the world. Today, I continue to learn from the *Course* and to *un*-learn some of my beliefs from the past.

I am now convinced that to be truly happy and peaceful, we must learn the value of forgiving and loving ourselves and others. Happiness and peace come about when we cease to look for someone or something to blame when things go wrong in our lives. Blaming cannot bring us the happiness we desire, nor can revenge and punishment. Only forgiveness can provide what we seek. We, therefore, must be the ones to stop recycling the anger, hurt, bitterness, and pain of both inside and outside wars.

As each of us takes responsibility for letting go of our own self-imposed blocks to forgiving others and ourselves, we become healed, joyful, and at peace.

Change Occurs by Overcoming One Obstacle at a Time

Overcoming fear, shame, and blame. The first obstacle we need to overcome is our unwillingness to change our belief systems. Perhaps the biggest block to forgiveness is having a belief system that is based on fear rather than love.* That block begins to vanish as we affirm a willingness in our lives to see other people either as being loving or as being fearful and giving a call of help for love. That means no longer interpreting other people's behavior to determine if they are guilty or innocent. It means seeing other people not as attacking but either as loving or as fearful and giving a call of help for love.

During most of my early life, I must admit that I certainly didn't see life this way. Like most people, I grew up with few, if any, models of forgiveness. Suddenly I was an adult with little awareness about what forgiveness could offer or how important it could be. When I was growing up, I heard about forgiveness, but it was only an abstract religious concept. I had no idea what it had to do with my own life. As far as I can remember, I was never taught anything about its practical application in my everyday life.

By the time I was in my twenties, I had become an expert at attacking or belittling myself and others. I looked for and found many people in the world who were more than willing to cooperate with me in this kind of behavior. In those days, my ego was like an automatic pilot, instantly switching on whenever I felt attacked. Once it switched on, God help anyone who happened to be in the line of fire! I would go instantly into my attack-and-defend mode.

I sometimes think that our life stories are the most powerful tools we have for passing along to others the lessons we ourselves have learned.

Any time I reflect on those difficult years and on what has happened since, I am reminded to have an open mind and to believe that nothing, truly nothing, is impossible. For that reason, I'd like to share the story about my divorce.

Surrendering to love instead of fear. In 1973, my first wife, Pat, and I divorced after a twenty-year marriage, and I found myself in emotional quicksand. I thrashed around in a mire of pain, shame, anger, blame, and frustration. I thought I would never get free. Most people who go through divorces know of what I speak.

The guilt, hostility, and self-blame that I was feeling dragged me down, exhausting me. I turned to alcohol for relief. I became an alcoholic and had a preoccupation with suicide. During those painful years, I believed that my relationship with Pat could never be healed. It seemed impossible to even imagine.

At the time, I had been an atheist for many years. The idea that I might one day be on a spiritual path seemed as unlikely as Pat and I ever being friends again. Then, in 1975, I became a student of the teachings of *A Course in*

Miracles. I noticed my belief system changing. Where once I had struggled to affix blame, guilt, and shame, all of that faded away. Soon I noticed that I was seeing myself and Pat very differently and was taking responsibility for all my thoughts and actions.

Every day I concentrated on seeing Pat in this new light. Rather than looking for who was to blame, I asked for God's help in forgiving myself and my now-ex-wife. I woke up each day with a single purpose—to have peace of mind, peace of God, as my only goal. Miraculously and unexpectedly, I soon noticed that the tension about Pat and our relationship was fading.

Pat remarried about a year later and moved to Seattle. Time passed, and one day I was booked to give a lecture at the Opera House in that city. Pat, her father, and her new husband came to hear my talk.

We met for breakfast the next morning, and Pat said she loved everything I had said. How very different our lives had become since our marriage!

Upon my return to San Francisco, I told everyone, "You know, this forgiveness stuff really works!" About six months later, I learned that Pat and her new husband were moving to Tiburon, where I lived.

My first response to this news was, "Oh, no!" It had been easy to be forgiving of Pat and myself when she was living several hundred miles away. But I wondered what would happen if we were bumping into each other from time to time at the grocery store.

During the years that followed, I realized how important it is to make forgiveness a continuous daily practice. I am happy to say that today, Pat and I are dear friends. The animosity of years past is gone. When Pat remarried, she asked that I take photos of her wedding and that my wife, Diane, do the videotaping. We did so with much pleasure. That day I was once again grateful for the miraculous impact of forgiveness that had touched all of our lives.

Becoming aware of perception and projection. As human beings we have a particular way of making sense of our lives. We have wonderful memories for everything that has ever happened to us, almost since the day of our births, and maybe before. If we have fearful or hurtful things happen to us when we are young, we not only remember them, but we tend to cling to them for judging the present and the future.

Our minds are like motion-picture projectors. Our memories of the past become the images we project out onto a screen. And the screen of our projections is often whatever person we are talking with at the moment. If the film running in our mind is one of guilt or anger, we are going to project those perceptions onto the present situation. We may see the other person as trying to make us feel guilty, or we may see them as deserving of our anger.

While perception and projection are part of being human, our egos are quite capable of using projection for their own purposes. They will convince us that what we are projecting onto other people from our own perceptions is true and real. The outcome is that our egos convince us that all our uncomfortable thoughts and feelings are caused by people or situations in the external world. The last thing our egos want us to know is that what we experience is determined by the thoughts in our own minds.

While we may not want to take responsibility for our own perceptions and projections, when we do so we are then able to make choices between the belief system of the ego and the belief system of love. As we become aware of how our egos use projection, we can make changes. We can honor our feelings and decide if we want to hang on to them or let them go.

When my sons were very young, I often got after them about cleaning up their rooms. Only many years later did I realize that my own office was quite untidy. Even though it made me uncomfortable for it to be that messy, I could not allow myself to be aware of it. Instead, my ego told me that all those feelings I had were the result of my sons' bad housekeeping habits.

Forgiving your ex-spouse. Several years ago, when I was giving a workshop for nurses working with people who had cancer, I took the group through an exercise in which I asked them to imagine a garbage can and then to imagine putting all their anger and guilt into it. After they had filled up the garbage can with these feelings, I asked them if they were willing to let those feelings go. Were they willing to forgive themselves and the persons who may have hurt them?

"If you are ready," I said, "imagine that you have a giant helium balloon. You tie it to the can and let it go. Then, watch the can raise slowly into the air, going higher and higher up into the sky until it has completely disappeared."

Most of the group did the exercise, but one nurse just stood at the back of the room and observed. I became involved with the others and did not notice her. During the break, however, she came rushing up to me to relate her experience.

"When you started the exercise," she told me, "I was certain there was nothing I felt angry or guilty about. So I decided I'd just watch. But all of a sudden I remembered my ex-husband, that *son of a bitch*! He left me for a younger woman. So, in my mind, I grabbed him by the neck and threw him into the garbage can. I fastened the imaginary balloon to the can and watched it disappear into the sky, exactly as you said. As it vanished into the clouds, I heard a loud pop in my neck. Just that suddenly, a pain that I'd had since our divorce was gone!"

She went on to tell me that she had then realized that it wasn't her ex-husband she got rid of but her attachment to her anger over what he had done. She said, "My husband was no longer a pain in the neck to me." She had seen her own anger at last and no longer had to project it onto other people.

Controlling past and future. To prepare our hearts and minds for forgiveness, we need to overcome the obstacle of believing that the past will inevitably be repeated in the future.

When we're attacked, fear puts us on guard. Even many years later we can find ourselves imprisoned by that fear, believing that we will be attacked like that again. Our egos tell us not to trust other people and even to expect them to attack us again. There's a part of us which lives in the fearful past, sure that it will repeat itself. There's a part of us which wants to adhere to the belief that the painful past can predict a painful future.

The belief in the past being a predictor of the future is held by the ego, which feeds on a steady diet of unforgiving thoughts, fear, judgment, blame, and guilt. But this same diet also keeps us separated from each other, from our true self, from the experience of love, and from the experience of the presence of God.

The symptoms of suffering and pain have their roots in our unforgiving thoughts and can take many different forms. Research into the psychophysiology of human stress has shown us that the thoughts and feelings we hold in our minds are frequently translated into physical symptoms or emotional disorders: anxiety, depression, agitation, poor self-esteem, headaches, backaches, pains in the neck, stomachaches, and compromised immunity that can make us prone to infection and allergies. It is time to stop attacking our bodies with our negative thoughts.

Our own judgments and unforgiving thoughts can also be translated into stress responses that literally attack our own bodies, becoming the underlying factors in the development of psycho-somatic symptoms of many kinds as well as actual organic diseases. Holding on to unforgiving thoughts thus has a very real effect on our general health.

Regardless of the description of the pain and suffering we experience, it is always wise to look for the presence of unforgiving thoughts that may be preventing us from healing.

We don't always like to accept the possibility that when we hold on to unforgiving thoughts, we are actually choosing to suffer. Our egos may be telling us that this is the way to punish the people who have hurt us, but we frequently injure only ourselves. Remember that pain, fear, uncertainty, and sickness all feed the ego. It abhors peace, love, happiness, and health.

Clinging to its usual weapons, our stubborn egos will tell us that it is OK to *sort of forgive*—but never to forgive totally. For instance, you can *sort of forgive* Uncle Harry for telling off-color jokes at your dinner party—but just to remind him that you don't forgive his rudeness totally, you don't send him a card on his birthday anymore.

Another way that our egos try to control our intention to forgive is by forgiving someone but maintaining our superiority in the process. For instance, you might tell Uncle Harry, "To keep peace in the family, I forgive you. But you really have a problem there, so don't think I'm not keeping an eye on you."

The ego perception we tend to believe is that if we don't continue to hold a grudge for someone who has hurt us, we put ourselves in danger. The trouble is that this kind of negative energy has a way of building up inside and boomeranging right back to us.

Remember that your thoughts and beliefs determine how you will experience your life.* The purpose of forgiveness is to release us from the past. It is to free us from the grudges and grievances we have with other people. Rather than putting us in danger, our forgiveness lets us live more fully in the present. The peaceful present, in turn, helps us to view the future with feelings of peace. The peaceful present can then extend into the future, where present and future become one. Unfortunately, most of us live in a reality where the fearful past and fearful future become the same, and our beliefs create a reality where the worst is yet to come.

Releasing obstacles of guilt and shame. In 1981, when I met Diane, I was writing a book titled *Good-bye to Guilt.* I had asked all my friends to share their stories about what they felt most guilty about in their lives.

When I asked Diane this question, she replied that there was nothing she felt guilty about. Later that day, she starting talking about her deceased father and found that she had been hiding her guilt, anger, and unforgiving thoughts even from herself.

She described how her father had been physically abusive. Diane herself was never beaten, but she said she felt guilty about wishing that her father had been different than he was. She also felt guilty because other people in her family were beaten, while she never was. As angry as she was at her father for his behavior, she had repressed her anger, burying it in a mental closet that remained unopened until that day.

Over the next week following her recollection of these events, she recalled many times in her childhood when she had played the role of the peacemaker. She had handled her feelings by holding them in and doing everything she could to keep peace in her family so that nobody would get hurt.

Now that she had opened up this storage of feelings, she began asking her Higher Power for help with forgiveness. One day, she felt guided to write a poem to her father. She has given her permission to share it with you in this book:

IF I COULD WALK WITH YOU, DAD

If I could walk with you, Dad,
A moment from time stolen free,
I'd feel the pace you walked,
And I'd find it soothing for me.

At the edge of day,
In the low August sun,
Weary from work,
And your chores to be done,

Your pleasures were small
And they seemed so worthless
To me.
Yet, as I reach each day,
It is they that set me free.

Your flowers, their gardens,
From baked clay you gave them
Life;
Your birds, their wings,
God's instruments in flight.

We spoke so little,
And we shared even less.
If I could walk with you, Dad,
My heart would confess
That I never understood your
Anger
Or your frustrations or your
Pain.
But as confusing as it was,
I have only gained.

Because you forced me to go
Inward,

To search and to find
The meaning of life,
Of love, and of time.

You taught me without teaching
And you gave me from inside
Many meanings to this journey
Though you never knew why.

You were my gardener,
And my tender, and my teacher
Untold,
From your heart and your
Hands,
My spirit you helped mold.

In my fragile cocoon,
Protected from strife,
I heard from inside
The meaning of life.

> *So I give to you now*
> *As we walk tonight, Dad*
> *My heart ... our connection*
> *Never again sad.*

For the past is gone
 And I have laid to rest,
 For we both know now
 We did our beautiful best.

 And I stand on the crest
 Of the hills of my mind
 And wave you on
 In your journey in time

 To find your family
 In Light, all around
 In love and peace and forgiveness
 May you always abound.

After writing this poem and talking about the feelings she was holding on to about her father, she found that healing could take place in an instant through forgiveness, even after a person has died. Forgiveness erased the shadow of the hurtful past, and she now has only loving memories of her dad, memories that previously were blocked.

Diane's experience shows us not only the power of forgiveness but also how we can heal our relationships with others even when the other person is either unavailable or deceased.

There have been many occasions during workshops or lectures when Diane has shared her poem and the story about her dad with our audiences. Many people have come up to thank Diane and tell her how much the poem helped them heal their relationships with their own fathers.

Other ways to forgive and heal. Diane's experience demonstrates how writing can be a powerful tool in the process of forgiveness and healing relationships. A poem, a letter to a friend, a page or two in a journal, and maybe even an unmailed letter to the person who has caused you pain all can provide you with a way to express feelings that you have found difficult but which need to be honored.

The fearful child that may still reside within you can be profoundly healed and assured of your love through the forgiveness process. To help with this, you may even want to find a baby picture of yourself and a photo of yourself when you were a child. Put the photos on your mirror, on your desk, or wherever you will see them often and be reminded of them. Love the fearful child you see in these photos every day, and you may find that the fearful child within you becomes a more joyful and loving adult.

*Forgiveness creates a world where we do not withhold our love from anyone.**

It becomes easier to forgive

when we choose to no longer

believe we are victims.

―――――――――

Forgiveness is a continuous process, not something we do just once or twice.

―――――――――

Six

Miracles of Forgiveness

Forgiving is the pathway to happiness and the quickest way to undo suffering and pain.*

Diane's story in the last chapter shows how quickly we can change something in ourselves when we become aware of it. This is important to realize, because we often hide the anger we feel from others as well as ourselves. That hidden anger becomes the thing that makes it so difficult for us to forgive. And our lack of forgiveness can eat us alive, creating tension that limits our relationships and attacks our bodies.

In this chapter, I'd like to explore some examples in which people have brought grievances from the past into their awareness and released them. It is my hope that these true stories might be helpful models that will guide others toward letting go of the past through forgiveness.

Healing the Scars of Religion

Many people throughout the world have been turned away from anything that resembles religion or God because of painful experiences they have had as children. In many ways, God gets a bad rap in our culture and is blamed for just about everything imaginable. We see this even in the policies of insurance companies that exclude payment for damages or injuries caused by "acts of God"—which usually means natural catastrophes such as floods, earthquakes, hurricanes, tornadoes, and forest fires caused by lightning. It is time for us to stop blaming God for all the terrible things that happen to us.

Recently we were having dinner with a woman who described herself as a "recovering Catholic." She told me that she had been raised in an orphanage and that she perceived this as a horrible experience about which she still felt much anger. She went on to describe in considerable detail some of the abuses she had suffered.

As an adult, she found herself repeating the same victim role again and again with pain and self-pity. She discovered that she was imprisoned by her own anger and by the rage she felt about being abandoned by her mother. Rather than protecting her from the past, her anger had become her jailer, causing her to repeat the past. She got angry every time she heard the words *religion* or *God*, seeing them as the cause of her pain.

In the past two years, however, she had begun to explore a spiritual path. She became increasingly aware of how she was blaming both God and religion for her feelings of abandonment and abuse. The more aware she became of this, the more she was able to see how she was responsible for holding on to the pain she was still feeling.

This woman has done a great deal of forgiving. Each day she feels greater freedom from the pain and anger associated with her past. There is a sparkle in her eye that was never there before, and she is beginning to experience happiness and even joy for the first time in her life. She no longer blames her parents or the church for her feelings. She is letting go of the painful perceptions that imprisoned her.

Make no mistake, however. She is not condoning the behavior of her parents or the people at the orphanage where she was sent to live. She in no way agrees that their behavior was OK. She finally realizes that it was only her own thoughts which were keeping her in agony. Forgiveness literally showed her the way to freedom.

This woman shares much with so many people I have known who, after healing past grievances, not only are able to experience once again the comfort of a spiritual connection with a Higher Power but even return to their original place of worship. Unfortunately, there are others who let their fights with God and religion dominate their lives with feelings of anger and lack of trust. We can discover in our feelings of blame a signal to awaken to the ways we have been clinging to past grievances and move forward to forgive them. By forgiving our misperceptions of God and by releasing God from blame, we open up new vistas for our personal fulfillment.

Forgiving Loved Ones Who Have Died

When someone close and dear to our heart dies, there can be a flood of emotions. The feelings of grief associated with losing that person's physical presence can be immense. Some of us deny our loss and grief by shedding no tears. Others may experience tears for months or even years.

Sometimes when a loved one dies after a prolonged and painful illness, family members and friends may feel relieved. Your ego may tell you that you should feel guilty for this feeling and that a "good person" would not have such emotions.

The loss of a loved one may cause us to feel angry at God and the world. We may or may not be aware of this anger. The ego may tell us that we should feel guilty about being angry.

I met a wonderful woman named Minnie at a workshop in Hawaii. Minnie told me that she was eighty-one years old and had not been able to stop crying for the past two years. It started when her son died at the age of forty-five. She had felt depressed and abandoned ever since.

A week before she came to the workshop, Minnie's counselor had told her that it was "time to stop crying and get on with your life."

Hearing these words, a little voice within my heart told me exactly what I was to say to Minnie. First, I reminded her that I was a doctor, and I told her that I was going to write a prescription for her. Her face brightened and she nodded. Then I took out a piece of paper and wrote, "It is all right for you to cry as much as you want and as often as you want, for the rest of your life." I signed my name and handed it to her.

Minnie's face lit up with a smile that went from ear to ear. It became clear to me that if I were to help her, all I had to do was give her my unconditional love and acceptance. She did not have to change for me to love her. I shared with her my personal belief that there really are no scripts for how a person should mourn or face death.

Many of the communication problems we have in life are the result of our having scripts that we want others to follow. Tearing up our scripts is a way to become happy.

Minnie was definitely feeling much better. I then asked her if she had a good imagination. She replied that she did. It was during a workshop break, so I looked around the room and found a man who looked to be about forty-five, the age when Minnie's son had died. I asked this person, whose name was Brad, if he would be willing to volunteer for a few moments to be Minnie's son, whose name was Franklin. Brad said he would be more than happy to do so.

I explained to Minnie that for the next ten minutes she could use her imagination to make it a reality that her son, Franklin, was actually in Brad's body at this time. She could say whatever she wanted to tell him, and Franklin would talk with her. She agreed to do it, and I proceeded to ask her if she had ever felt angry at Franklin for leaving her. She paused for a second and then said, "Yes, I certainly have!" She shared some of the feelings she had around the anger.

I coached Brad on what to say. As Franklin, he told Minnie that he was fine and that he was with her in spirit all of the time. He said, "We do not have to be in bodies to communicate. Our minds can communicate without a physical presence."

Now Franklin, through Brad, went on to say that when we know we are joined as one with God and each other, there is only joy. He assured Minnie that she would never be alone because she could always choose to experience his presence and God's presence whenever she wished.

Minnie stopped crying almost immediately upon hearing these words. She pressed her head to her son's (Franklin's) chest. In a little while she was able to tell him, "I forgive you for dying."

Minnie's body energy shifted dramatically. A great weight had been lifted from her shoulders. She was all lightness and smiles.

About an hour later, Minnie came over to me and said that she no longer felt like weeping.

"That's great," I said. "But it is still just fine for you to cry all you want."

As the workshop was breaking up later that afternoon, Minnie came up to me and said, "Jerry, someone told me you like to dance. Is that right?"

"I do!" I said, "I love to dance."

With a gleam in her eye, Minnie told me about a dance that would be taking place. Would I be interested in going?

I told her I would love to. And so we went out dancing and had a great time. Not only was this a wonderful lesson in the power of forgiveness, but it was also another confirmation that giving truly is receiving.

Forgiveness in Our Work Lives

Relationships in the workplace present a special challenge for most employers as well as employees. Jealousies, fear of rejection, fear of being honest, and a host of other problems can occur. Sometimes the stress in our work relationships can result in physical symptoms. It is as if we turn the anger we have toward another person inward, attacking ourselves. Here's an example:

I was invited to give a lecture to a group in Canada. The woman who was the executive director of the organization to which I would be talking had a severe gallbladder attack, was in great pain, and was not going to be able to attend. In fact, she was waiting for a hospital room to go in for surgery.

Mary could hardly speak to me because of the pain. I asked her if she would like me to give her some relaxation exercises to try. She said she would. After a few minutes, she began to relax and the pain diminished somewhat.

As we talked, she shared what had been going on in her life just before the gallbladder attack. She had worked in a doctor's office for the last fifteen years. Six months earlier, the physician who was her employer had asked her to take down some paintings his sister had done and find some new ones.

This was good news for Mary, who disliked the old paintings. But they hadn't been down for long when the doctor's sister came to town and talked him into putting them back up. Mary was so angry that she quit on the spot.

Until we talked, Mary had made no association between these events, her anger, and her gallbladder attack. Suddenly she made the connection. She said she wanted to honor her anger but definitely didn't want to hang on to it.

We began doing some forgiveness exercises, and within twenty minutes the pain was gone. She felt well enough to go to the conference the next day, and her doctor agreed that this would be OK.

At the conference, Mary shared her story of how her gallbladder attack was associated with her anger and how her forgiveness released her from the pain she had been experiencing. In the weeks following the conference, she completed her forgiveness with her employer and returned to work with him.

Celestial Amnesia Is Remembering Only Love

In our work lives, it can be extremely helpful to have a forgiveness process that is easy to do whenever we feel the need. You simply imagine that someone has given you a medicine that will give you a selective form of amnesia which lasts for ten minutes. It can be helpful if you imagine that this special medicine is in a glass of water which you drink. During the ten-minute period that this medicine is in effect, you forget all hurtful memories of the past; you remember only memories of love.

By focusing only on this remembered love, most people feel themselves become peaceful and joyful, living very much in the present moment.

No matter where you are, remember that forgiveness offers you peace of mind and everything else you could possibly ever want or hope for. It is an elixir, giving you your wholeness and leading you into the heart of God and into oneness with our Creator.

Forgiveness in Times of Disaster

In 1989, a very destructive earthquake hit San Francisco, and many people lost their homes. One family that lost their home moved across the bay to the Oakland hills. A few years later, a terrible fire swept through this area and their home was destroyed again.

It would be easy for anyone who had experienced such disasters to feel victimized and to get stuck in self-pity. But this family was different. They honored their feelings, and they forgave what seemed to be happening to them in their lives. They recognized that what had occurred was beyond their explanation, and rather than getting caught up in being victims, they moved on in their lives.

Hardly a week goes by when somewhere in our world there are not natural disasters that cause great hardship to people. Many families might feel themselves victims and hold on to their grievances for the rest of their lives. How did the family above heal? They found that asking *why* didn't help. The answer to that question might remain a mystery forever. To heal from such disasters, we have to ask *what*, not why. What can I learn from this situation? What can I do to move forward? What did I learn from this situation that will help me in the future?

When disasters of this kind occur in extremely poor countries, some people's possessions may be limited to a bowl of rice and the meager clothes on their back. They truly know that at such times it is the preciousness of life itself and the love of family and friends that count the most.

Forgiving a Country

The biographies of Anwar Sadat, Mahatma Gandhi, Martin Luther King Jr., and Nelson Mandela, as well as a host of others like them, tell us how they found their way to forgiveness while they were in jail. They acknowledged and honored their feelings of bitterness, anger, and vengeance. But forgiveness helped them transform these feelings into positive actions for change when they finally got out of jail.

As history shows, their forgiveness did not mean that they condoned or agreed with those who jailed them. They came to realize that the real jail is in our minds when we are full of fear, anger, and deep grievance. They moved beyond these feelings to begin bringing about the social changes they stood for.

We have a close and dear friend, Henri Landwirth, who was a prisoner at Auschwitz and other concentration camps during World War II. There was a time when he thought it would be impossible to ever forgive those who had been so cruel to him and to millions of others. Henri later changed his mind. He had seen life at its worst. He was almost killed and came close to dying from starvation many times.

When Henri came to the United States after the war, his heart was filled with hatred for the German government. He thought these feelings would never leave him. Both his parents had been murdered under Nazi rule.

He became very successful in business in this country and started a philanthropic organization called Give Kids the World. This organization makes it possible for children who have life-threatening illnesses to visit Disney World in Orlando, Florida. Over seven thousand children come to the village each year. For many children, Give Kids the World acts as a bridge to heaven.

Henri told me that holding on to his hatred of the German soldiers who had committed atrocities was killing him. But his heart was transformed by working so closely with children through Give Kids the World. It has been a gradual process, but he states that today he has forgiven Germany and those who committed heinous atrocities. He states that he no longer wants to continue recycling the anger.

Last year, Henri and seven other Holocaust survivors were invited to speak at a dinner honoring Holocaust victims. Most survivors talked about their continued anger and hatred of the past. Henri was the last to speak. He talked about all his blessings since coming to the United States. He spoke of how grateful he is for the love he continues to receive. He emphasized how important it is to live in the present, not to be stuck in the past.

Forgiving Institutions

Since the time that Yeltsin took over from Gorbachev in Russia, relations have become more harmonious between our two countries. At a cocktail party I was attending there, one of the Russian officials said to me, "Now that our two countries are at peace, I think the United States will have to go out and find a new enemy." I thought his remark had a lot of merit.

When we follow the ego's creed, we are always looking for a new enemy. We no sooner heal one relationship conflict than a new one pops up. It sometimes appears that we cannot live our lives without at least one enemy to fight.

In the United States, the Internal Revenue Service becomes an easy institution to hate and make into our enemy. There are horror stories of individuals and businesses who have been ruined by the agency's heavy-handed tactics. While legislators promise us that new laws are being written to prevent IRS abuses, there continue to be people whose rage at the IRS is so high that they are considering moving to another country.

It is very easy for us to be angry at the IRS. We can point to things they have done that seem to *justify* our anger. Besides, there are always people around us who are equally angry and will support what we are feeling. It is human and understandable to be angry in situations like this. It is our attachment to the anger that gets us into trouble.

Some people I know have let go of their rage at institutions such as this. They have let go of their need to punish them, have forgiven, and have moved on in peace. Again, forgiving—whether forgiving a close friend or a whole society—does not take away the responsibility of the persons who have done things that inflicted hardship, death, or emotional pain. Forgiving does not mean condoning such behavior.

Above all, forgiveness is the process of letting go of your attachment to the negative thoughts in your mind. It is the process of healing your own mind and your own soul.

Is it possible to believe that we can live in this world without needing to believe we have enemies? Whenever I ask myself this question, I remember a Pogo comic strip in which one of the characters says, "We have met the enemy and it is us."

Perhaps, as Pogo suggests, we will no longer have enemies the day we all choose to forgive the past and live wholly in the present. And on this day we will discover that it was only our lack of forgiveness which kept us chained to the painful past.

Forgiving the Military

Our egos have the capacity to put us in a vise of conflict and blame around any person, place, or institution. Forgiveness, on the other hand, is like a key unlocking us from the shackles of our egos.

Sometimes, as in the following story, we hide our grudges so deeply in the caverns of our minds that we have no awareness of the judgments and grievances we've left smoldering there.

In 1979, my friend Dr. Bill Thetford and I were invited to give a seminar on forgiveness at Travis Air Force Base in Northern California. As we were driving to the lecture, I started feeling increasingly uncomfortable. Finally, I told Bill that I was going to pull over to the side of the road. I had to talk.

"Bill," I said, "how can I give a seminar on forgiveness when I am holding such a strong grievance against the military, where we are going to be talking?"

During the Korean conflict, I was pulled out of my child psychiatry residency to put in time at Travis. Every bone in my body had resisted. I was against killing or injuring people in any way, for any reason. Under no circumstances did I want to serve an organization that thought it was OK, under some circumstances, to kill people.

"I am still holding on to feelings of resentment and anger at the military for forcing me to serve them against my will." I told Bill that I was still clinging to those judgmental feelings and was not at all peaceful. There was a war going on inside me.

I asked Bill to meditate with me as I attempted to let go of these feelings, forgive, and come back to the present without all that baggage from my past. It worked! Soon I was peaceful, and we gave a very successful workshop. I had none of the old, negative feelings I once held in my mind for the military.

Forgiveness allows us to experience our wholeness, our oneness with all of life. It opens our eyes to experience the light and the essence of love that we all are.

Forgiveness is like getting pregnant. Either you are pregnant or you're not. Nor can you ever "sort of forgive." Sort of forgiving just doesn't work; it has to be total and complete.

It is always helpful to take a new look at the people and situations that we have not forgiven. Ask yourself if there is value or harm for you to persist to hold on to those old grievances.

The process of forgiving has no set structure or form. The person you are forgiving need not change at all. For that matter, they may never change! The only requirement is your willingness to change the thoughts in your own mind.

Forgiving Ourselves

The staff at the Center for Attitudinal Healing in Sausalito, California, had joined Diane and me at a workshop in Hawaii. During part of the workshop, the group divided up into pairs. Two partners would sit facing each other. Then one person would tell the other something they would like to forgive about themselves. The person listening would do their best to not make any judgments and to hold a space of unconditional love.

When it came my turn to talk about something I had not forgiven about myself, I could not think of anything. All of a sudden something popped into my head. I told the compassionate and understanding woman sitting opposite me that I had set a schedule for myself to do the final editing of a book I was writing. I wasn't aware that I had been measuring myself and my progress, but at that moment I realized that I was giving myself a failing grade.

I finished telling my story, and by the end of it I had already forgiven myself for my negative judgments. It was like frosting on the cake to hear my partner say, "I forgive you."

Curious, my partner then asked me, "What is the title of the book you are working on?"

I barely got the words out before we both burst out laughing. The book I was working on is the one you are holding in your hands— *Forgiveness: The Greatest Healer of All*.

So even though I have written this book on forgiveness, I still have my temptations and challenges. Perhaps as long as we remain in these bodies we will be tempted to judge and not forgive. We will forever need to remind ourselves that each new moment is an opportunity to choose once again. I am convinced that one of the greatest gifts of all is our power to choose the thoughts we want to put in our minds. The freedom to choose can release us from our self-imposed jail cells. It can release us from the enemy Pogo discovered—ourselves and our own attachment to the past.

Forgiveness puts us in the flow of love. The result of our forgiveness is a reminder that love is our only reality, that love is everything and everywhere. Love is all there is, and it is the answer to every problem or question that we may ever have to face.

Forgiving a Child and a School Principal

I am convinced that we will have a society which is focused more on cooperation than on competition when we begin expressing love and forgiveness in our homes and schools. When we believe that love and forgiveness can produce miracles, they begin to occur.

In 1998, Diane and I went to West Africa to consult with the Center for Attitudinal Healing in Accra. While we were there, the executive director of the center, Mary Clottey, told us this story:

Mary is a teacher at a school located about two hours from the capital. In her teaching she spent a great deal of time helping her young students find ways to communicate with each other without anger and fighting. She emphasized the process of forgiveness. In fact, her students knew her as "the forgiveness teacher."

There was a ten-year-old boy in the school who was a real terror. He fought with everyone and disrupted everything around him. Wherever he went, he seemed to break things, though he never accepted any responsibility for what he did.

One day he was caught red-handed stealing money from his teacher's purse. The school principal jumped in and called for an assembly. According to the tradition of the school, the boy would be whipped with a cane up on the stage where everyone in the school could watch. They would make an example of him in this way, and then he would be expelled.

The entire school assembled in the auditorium where the caning was to take place. But as the boy was led out to be caned, Mary stood up. Just as she was about to say, "Forgive him," all the children around her leapt to their feet.

"Forgive him! Forgive him! Forgive him!" the children chanted, until the whole assembly hall was ringing with the message.

The boy stared out into the audience and then broke down and began to sob. Suddenly the whole climate of the assembly hall changed.

In the end, the boy was never caned. Nor was he expelled. Instead, he was forgiven and loved. From that day forward, he has not gotten into a single fight, broken anything, stolen, or been disruptive in any way.

At first, many people in the school believed that the principal's action of calling the assembly to punish the boy was harsh and unfair. But he was forgiven, too, and in the process the seeds were planted for a new, more loving environment in the school.

Forgiveness in the Community

Here is another story about forgiveness that comes from Africa. When a person acts unjustly or irresponsibly in the Babemba tribe of South Africa, he is placed alone in the center of the village but is in no way prevented from running off.

Everyone in the village stops working and gathers in a circle around the person who has been accused. Then each person, regardless of age, begins to tell the person in the center about all the good things he or she has done during his or her life.

Everything that can be remembered about this person is described in great detail. All the accused's positive attributes, good deeds, strengths, and kindnesses are verbalized for their benefit. Each person in the circle does this in great detail.

All the stories about this person are told with the utmost sincerity and love. No one is allowed to exaggerate events that happened, and everyone knows that they cannot make stories up. Nobody is insincere or sarcastic as they speak.

This ceremony continues until everyone in the village has had his or her say about how they value this person as a respected member of their community. This process can go on for several days. In the end, the tribe breaks the circle, and a joyous celebration occurs as the person is welcomed back into the tribe.

Through the eyes of love, which this ceremony so beautifully describes, we find only reunion and forgiveness. Each person in the circle, as well as the person who is standing in the center, is reminded that forgiveness gives us the opportunity to let go of the past and the fearful future. The person in the center is no longer labeled as a bad person or excluded from the community. Instead, they are reminded of the love that is within them and are joined with those around them.

Forgiveness between Brothers

Often our most difficult conflicts and grievances are with family members who we feel have done something unforgivable. Several years ago, while I was giving a lecture in Honolulu, a middle-aged man wearing a business suit came up to me and asked if we could talk.

Everyone else in the room was wearing Hawaiian shirts and casual clothes, so I suspected he might be a physician—which he was. He told me that he and his brother had not spoken for six years. Their relationship had ended with an argument. He explained that he had read my book *Love Is Letting Go of Fear*, and because he had begun seeing the value of forgiveness, he had decided to give his brother a call.

The physician told me that he had called his brother and told him he would like to let go of the past, to let bygones be bygones. The two men agreed to get together the following week. At lunch that day, everything was peaceful, and there was no reference made to their past argument. Instead, their love for each other radiated from their table.

The physician thanked me because he felt that if he hadn't read my book, he never would have had the lunch meeting that day. It was doubly important to him, because a week later his brother was killed in an auto accident. What a wonderful reminder this story is that it is never too early or to late to forgive!

About ten years after this story was told to me, I was referred to a physician for a consultation about a health issue I was having. When I entered his office, the physician introduced himself and asked if I remembered him. I had to confess that I didn't. He then said, "I am the man who told you about the experience I had with forgiving my brother." I was thrilled to be able to thank him once again for his story, which I had shared with thousands of people over the years.

Guidelines of Forgiveness

It is my hope and belief that you might use the stories in this chapter as examples and guidelines for how forgiveness can work in our lives. In the following chapter, I outline preparatory as well as action steps for the forgiveness process.

Forgiveness is the

shortest route to God.

Forgiveness is the eraser that makes

the hurtful past disappear.

Forgiving can be a most important

process not only for a person

who is dying but for the people

who are left behind.

Seven

Stepping Stones to Forgiveness

Let peace of mind be your only goal—
not changing the other person
*or punishing them.**

The Preparation Stage: Changing Our Beliefs

Preparation for retraining our minds begins with learning to quiet them so that we are not caught up in the busyness of the day. Prayer can be helpful for this. If you meditate, you might start there.

Meditation simply means having a peaceful mind. You may have had the experience of hiking in the mountains and coming upon a quiet lake so clear and pure you could see the bottom. Let that image or a similar one be your symbol for a peaceful mind.

A peaceful mind is our natural state, one that is tranquil, still, joyous, and loving. Its clarity becomes possible because there are no conflicting thoughts, judgments, or fears.

To have a peaceful mind, find an image like the mountain lake that will work for you. Then spend between five and twenty minutes each day focusing on that image in a place where you will not be disturbed by other people, the ringing phone, or anything else.

Finding time to be in nature and experience your oneness with it can be most helpful. Just be quiet, and have nothing to distract you—no television, radio, or talking. Turn off your phone. The stillness you create will help you be more receptive to the different ways of looking at forgiveness.

I have included in this chapter a list of principles that we have already discussed. Don't let the size of this list bother you. Be gentle and patient with yourself. Resist any temptation you might have to compare yourself to others or to measure your progress. Find a space that is comfortable and natural for you, and honor it.

Have a willingness to be open-minded as you review these principles. Remind yourself that it is all right to disagree with or reject any of these thoughts. Forgiveness is a choice, and you do not have to forgive or believe in forgiveness. But do your best to look at the consequences of your choice to forgive or not forgive, letting your heart help you decide.

- Be open to the possibility of changing your beliefs about forgiveness.

- Be willing to consider that you are not just a body but that you are a spiritual being living temporarily in a body.

- Consider the possibility that life and love are one and are eternal.

- Find no value in self-pity.

- Find no value in being a faultfinder.

- Choose to be happy rather than "right."

- Be willing to let go of being a victim.

- Make peace of mind your only goal.

- Look upon everyone you meet as a teacher of forgiveness.

- Believe that holding on to grievances and unforgiving thoughts is a way for you to suffer.

- Recognize that any emotional pain you feel at this moment is caused only by your own thoughts.

- Believe that you have the power to choose the thoughts you put in your mind.

- Believe that holding on to anger does not bring you what you really want.

- Believe that it is to your benefit to make decisions based on love rather than fear.

- Believe that there is no value in punishing yourself.

- Believe you deserve to be happy.

- Rather than seeing people as attacking you, see them as fearful and giving you a call of help for love.

- Be willing to see the light of an innocent child in everyone you meet, regardless of the costumes they wear and regardless of the terrible things that they have done.

- Be willing to see the light of the innocent child within you.

- Be willing to count your blessings rather than your hurts.

- Seek the value of giving up all your judgments.

- Believe that love is the most powerful healing force in the world.

- Believe that everyone you meet is a teacher of patience.

- Believe that forgiveness is the key to happiness.

- Believe that you can experience "celestial amnesia," momentarily forgetting everything except the love that others have given you.

- Recognize that every meeting you have, with every person you meet, is a Holy Encounter. Imagine that the person you are meeting is really Jesus, Buddha, Mohammed, Mother Teresa, or some other wise spiritual teacher who is within the personality you are dealing with. No matter how it might seem, treat this as a sacred relationship in which there is an opportunity to learn.

- Let go of seeing any value in hurting or punishing the other person or yourself. Remember that the purpose of forgiveness is not to change the other person but to change the conflicting, negative thoughts in your mind.

The Action Stage: Choosing to Forgive

One key word, *willingness*, gives you the power to move ahead in the forgiveness process. When you go into action and say to yourself, with full trust, that you are willing to turn all your grievances and what may seem like justified anger over to the highest truth in yourself—a Higher Power, God, or whatever name you apply in speaking of your Source—your anger will begin to be transformed into love. It is your willingness to seek help from this Higher Power that allows you to transform your anger into love.

- Decide that you are no longer going to suffer from the *boomerang effect* of your unforgiving thoughts.

- You may find it helpful to write a letter to the person you wish to forgive. Express all of your feelings, and then tear up the letter.

- You may find it healing in the forgiveness process to write poetry. Put your thoughts and feelings into intimate and well-expressed words.

- Be clear that your only goal is peace of mind, not changing or punishing the other person.

- Be willing to see this person who hurt you as one of your strongest teachers, giving you the opportunity to really learn what forgiveness is all about.

- Remember that in the process of forgiving the other person, you are forgiving yourself.

- Begin to practice and find the value of blessing and praying for the other person as well as yourself.

- Remember that in forgiving, you are not agreeing with the other person or condoning their hurtful behavior.

- Enjoy the happiness and peace that comes from forgiving.

_____

Gentleness and tenderness are the

brothers and sisters of forgiveness.

_____

Forgiveness makes our

load in life much lighter.

It is never too early

or too late to forgive.

EPILOGUE

When we each take responsibility for removing the blocks to the presence of love through forgiveness, what we will experience is going to be peace, joy, and happiness that is beyond our imagination.

Forgiveness is the bridge to God, love, and happiness. It is the bridge that allows us to say good-bye to guilt, blame, and shame. It teaches us that love is letting go of fear.

Forgiveness clears the air and purifies the heart and soul. It puts us in touch with all that is sacred. Through forgiveness, we connect with that which is greater than ourselves, with that which is beyond our imagination and full understanding. It allows us to be peaceful with the mystery of life. It creates the opportunity for us to do what we came here to do:

Teach Only Love, for That Is What We Are.

In closing this book, I'd like to share with you a poem I wrote in Bosnia in 1998 while Diane and I were on our way to a workshop titled "Forgiveness and Reconciliation for Religious and Spiritual Leaders."

You may want to read this poem weekly as a way of reviewing some of the forgiveness principles in this book.

FORGIVENESS

To forgive is the prescription
     For happiness.

To not forgive is the prescription
     To suffer.

Is it possible
     All pain

Regardless of its cause
Has some component of
Unforgiveness in it?

To hold on to vengeful thoughts
  To withhold our love and compassion
  Certainly must interfere
  With our health
  And our immune system.

Holding on to what we call justified anger
  Interferes with our experiencing
  The Peace of God.

To forgive
  Does not mean
  Agreeing with the act;
  It does not mean condoning
  An outrageous behavior.

Forgiveness means
  No longer living in
  The fearful past.

Forgiveness means
> *No longer scratching wounds*
> *So they continue to bleed.*

Forgiveness means
> *Living and loving*
> *Completely in the present,*
> *Without the shadows of the past.*

Forgiveness means
> *Freedom from anger*
> *And attack thoughts.*

Forgiveness means
> *Letting go of all hopes*
> *For a better past.*

Forgiveness means
> *Not excluding*
> *Your love from anyone.*

Forgiveness means
> *Healing the hole in your heart*
> *Caused by unforgiving thoughts.*

Forgiveness means
  Seeing the light of God
  In everyone, regardless
  Of their behavior.

Forgiveness is not just for
  The other person—but for ourselves
  And the mistakes we have made,
  And the guilt and shame we still hold on to.

Forgiveness in the deepest sense
  Is forgiving ourselves
  For separating ourselves from a loving God.

Forgiveness means
  Forgiving God and our
  Possible misperceptions of God
  That we have ever been
  Abandoned or left alone.

To forgive this very instant
  Means no longer being
  King or Queen of the Procrastinators' Club.

Forgiveness opens the door
For our feeling joined in Spirit
As one with everyone
And everyone with God.

It is never too early
To forgive.
It is never too late
to forgive.

How long does it take
to forgive?

It depends on your belief system.

If you believe it will never happen,
It will never happen.

If you believe it will take six months,
It will take six months.

If you believe it will take but a second,
That's all that it will take.

I believe with all my heart
That peace will come to the world
When each of us takes the
Responsibility of forgiving everyone,
Including ourselves, completely.

Other Books by Gerald G. Jampolsky, M.D.

Love Is Letting Go of Fear

•

*To Give Is to Receive: An Eighteen Day Mini-Course
on Healing Relationships*

•

*Teach Only Love: The Seven Principles
of Attitudinal Healing*

•

*Good-bye to Guilt:
Releasing Fear through Forgiveness*

•

*Out of Darkness into the Light:
A Journey of Inner Healing*

•

*One Person Can Make a Difference:
Ordinary People Doing Extraordinary Things*

With Diane V. Cirincione, Ph.D.

*Love Is the Answer:
Creating Positive Relationships*

Change Your Mind, Change Your Life:
Concepts in Attitudinal Healing

•

"Me First" and the Gimme Gimmes: A Story of Love
and Forgiveness, Choices and Changes

•

Wake-up Calls

With Lee L. Jampolsky, Ph.D.

Listen to Me: A Book for Men and Women About
Father-Son Relationships

Audiocassettes

Love Is Letting Go of Fear

•

Teach Only Love

•

Good-bye to Guilt

•

To Give Is to Receive

•

Love Is the Answer:
Creating Positive Relationships

Forgiveness Is the Key to Happiness

•

Introduction to
A Course in Miracles

•

One Person Can Make a Difference

•

The Quiet Mind

•

Achieving Inner Peace

•

Visions of the Future

•

Finding the Miracle of Love
in Your Life: Based on
A Course in Miracles

Videocassettes

Achieving Inner and Outer Success

•

Healing Relationships

Visions of the Future

For information about the Center for Attitudinal Healing in Sausalito, California, and its workshops, or about other centers, or about the lectures and workshops of Jerry Jampolsky and Diane Cirincione, please contact the Center for Attitudinal Healing, 33 Buchanan Drive, Sausalito, CA 94965; phone: (415) 331-6161; fax: (415) 331-4545.

If you wish to purchase books and audio- or videotapes, please contact Miracle Distributions, 1141 E. Ash Ave., Fullerton, CA 92631; phone: 1-800-359-2246; or contact the Sausalito Center for Attitudinal Healing.

Other Books from
Beyond Words Publishing, Inc.

Healing Your Rift with God
A Guide to Spiritual Renewal and Ultimate Healing
Author: Paul Sibcy
$14.95, softcover

God, says Paul Sibcy, is everything that is. All of us—faithful seekers or otherwise—have some area of confusion, hurt, or denial around this word, or our personal concept of God, that keeps us from a full expression of our spirituality. *Healing Your Rift with God* is a guidebook for finding our own personal rifts with God and healing them. Sibcy explains the nature of a spiritual rift, how this wound can impair our lives, and how such a wound may be healed by the earnest seeker, with or without help from a counselor or teacher. *Healing Your Rift with God* will also assist those in the helping professions who wish to facilitate what the author calls ultimate healing. The book includes many personal stories from the author's life, teaching, and counseling work, and its warm narrative tone creates an intimate author–reader relationship that inspires the healing process.

Rites of Passage

Celebrating Life's Changes

Authors: Kathleen Wall, Ph.D., and Gary Ferguson

$12.95, softcover

Every major transition in our lives—be it marriage, high-school graduation, the death of a parent or spouse, or the last child leaving home—brings with it opportunities for growth and self-actualization and for repositioning ourselves in the world. Personal ritual—the focus of *Rites of Passage*—allows us to use the energy held within the anxiety of change to nourish the new person that is forever struggling to be born. *Rites of Passage* begins by explaining to readers that human growth is not linear, as many of us assume, but rather occurs in a five-part cycle. After sharing the patterns of transition, the authors then show the reader how ritual can help him or her move through these specific life changes: work and career, intimate relationships, friends, divorce, changes within the family, adolescence, issues in the last half of life, and personal loss.

Watermelon Magic

Seeds of Wisdom, Slices of Life

Author: Wally Amos, $14.95 softcover

Watermelon Magic is an inspirational/motivational book using watermelons as a metaphor for life. Utilizing the life experiences of Wally Amos, the book shows the parallels between watermelons and humans. *Watermelon Magic* tells how Wally Amos uses his faith in everyday life and the wisdom gained from the past to help him make wise choices. Just as the vine connects the watermelons, we are all connected by spirit. And just as prickly vines make it difficult to get the melons, our human connections are sometimes prickly, making it difficult for us to achieve our goals and realize our dreams. *Watemelon Magic* helps us acknowledge the difficulties and choose a path to success.

The Great Wing
A Parable
Author: Louis A. Tartaglia, M.D.
Foreword: Father Angelo Scolozzi
$14.95, hardcover

The Great Wing transforms the timeless miracle of the migration of a flock of geese into a parable for the modern age. It recounts a young goose's own reluctant but steady transformation from gangly fledgling to Grand Goose and his triumph over the turmoils of his soul and the buffeting of a mighty Atlantic storm. In *The Great Wing*, our potential as individuals is affirmed, as is the power of group prayer, or the "Flock Mind." As we make the journey with this goose and his flock, we rediscover that we tie our own potential into the power of the common good by way of attributes such as honesty, hope, courage, trust, perseverance, spirituality, and service. The young goose's trials and tribulations, as well as his triumph, are our own.

Divine Intervention
A Journey from Chaos to Clarity
Author: Susan Anderson
Foreword: David Lukoff, Ph.D.
Afterword: Emma Bragdon, Ph.D.
$13.95, softcover

Divine Intervention is a powerfully written and engaging story of spiritual transformation. Susan Anderson's journey from chaos to clarity provides hope and inspiration for anyone facing the challenge of a major crisis or life change. Susan's spiritual emergency causes her to reconnect with her true self and experience an authentic sense of fulfillment and joy that could only be created by a *Divine Intervention*. Having received rave reviews from doctors, spiritual leaders, and lay readers, this book is a treasure of insight and wisdom that will empower women and men to take charge of their lives. For those wanting to help anyone in a spiritual emergency, also included is a guide and resource directory by Emma Bragdon, Ph.D., author of *Sourcebook for Helping People in Spiritual Emergency*.

A Life Worth Living

Recording Your Values, Memories, Goals, and Dreams
Author: Jerry Hawley
$19.95, hardcover

To provide a record of what each of us has done and where we are going, we created *A Life Worth Living*. The book is a living legacy for families to share for generations, and it includes pockets for mementos, blank pages to write affirmations, lots of questions for reflection, and an envelope for special treasures. Like Jimmy Stewart in the movie *It's a Wonderful Life*, few of us realize how our lives impact the people around us. Few of us record the details of our lives so that our children and grandchildren can know who we are, what has made our lives unique, who our friends are, what we have accomplished, and who touched our lives in memorable ways. Imagine the joy of discovering fascinating things about the lives of your parents and grandparents when you read what they have written in *A Life Worth Living*.

The Intuitive Way

A Guide to Living from Inner Wisdom
Author: Penney Peirce; Foreword: Carol Adrienne
$16.95, softcover

When intuition is in full bloom, life takes on a magical, effortless quality; your world is suddenly full of synchronicities, creative insights, and abundant knowledge just for the asking. *The Intuitive Way* shows you how to enter that state of perceptual aliveness and integrate it into daily life to achieve greater natural flow through an easy-to-understand, ten-step course. Author Penney Peirce synthesizes teachings from psychology, East-West philosophy, religion, metaphysics, and business. In simple and direct language, Peirce describes the intuitive process as a new way of life and demonstrates many practical applications from speeding decision-making to expanding personal growth. Whether you're just beginning to search for a richer, fuller life experience or are looking for more subtle, sophisticated insights about your spiritual path, *The Intuitive Way* will be your companion as you progress through the stages of intuition development.

Questions for My Father
Finding the Man Behind Your Dad
Author: Vin Staniforth
$15.00, hardcover

Questions for My Father is a little book that asks big questions—some serious, some playful, some risky. Each question is an opportunity to open, rejuvenate, or bring closure to the powerful but often overlooked relationship between fathers and children.

Fathers have long been regarded as objects of mystery and fascination. *Questions for My Father* provides a blueprint for uncovering the full dimensions of the man behind the mystery. It offers a way to let fathers tell their personal stories and to let children explore their own knowledge and understanding of one of the largest figures in their lives. In rediscovering their dad, readers will discover themselves.

To order or to request a catalog, contact
Beyond Words Publishing, Inc.
20827 N.W. Cornell Road, Suite 500
Hillsboro, OR 97124-9808
503-531-8700

You can also visit our Web site at *www.beyondword.com* or e-mail us at *info@beyondword.com*.

Beyond Words Publishing, Inc.

Our Corporate Mission:

Inspire to Integrity

Our Declared Values:

We give to all of life as life has given us.
We honor all relationships.
Trust and stewardship are integral to fulfilling dreams.
Collaboration is essential to create miracles.
Creativity and aesthetics nourish the soul.
Unlimited thinking is fundamental.
Living your passion is vital.
Joy and humor open our hearts to growth.
It is important to remind ourselves of love.